LOVE
on the
WING

LOVE
on the
WING

Maxine Lantz

WestBow Press
PRESS
A DIVISION OF THOMAS NELSON

WestBow Press books may be ordered through booksellers or by contacting:

WestBow Press
A Division of Thomas Nelson
1663 Liberty Drive
Bloomington, IN 47403
www.westbowpress.com
1-(866) 928-1240

Because of the dynamic nature of the Internet, any web addresses or links contained in this book may have changed since publication and may no longer be valid. The views expressed in this work are solely those of the author and do not necessarily reflect the views of the publisher, and the publisher hereby disclaims any responsibility for them.

Certain stock imagery © Thinkstock.
Any people depicted in stock imagery provided by Thinkstock are models, and such images are being used for illustrative purposes only.

ISBN: 978-1-4497-5628-4 (e)
ISBN: 978-1-4497-5627-7(sc)

Library of Congress Control Number: 2012910515

Printed in the United States of America

WestBow Press rev. date: 9/21/2012

AUTHOR'S FOREWORD

I have called this booklet of poetry "Love On The Wing" because it is from God's great love and care for me that I can soar and fly. The hearts on this cover symbolize that great love, and the butterflies symbolize the change in my life since I accepted the Lord as my Savior.

I hope that these poems will give you some insight into what I believe is the true character of God and his son, Jesus Christ. I thank God for saving me, and I look forward to spending eternity with God and Jesus Christ.

I pray that these poems will edify the reader, and that those who know Christ as Saviour will be encouraged to continue their walk with him. For the reader that does not yet know Christ in this personal way, I pray that these words will lead you to the point in your life where you will accept Christ as your personal Saviour.

I would also like to take this opportunity to thank the keepers of my words. Each poem I write gets sent to my sister (Lynda Taylor), my husband Jim, my pastor and his wife (John & Cheryl Scorgie, who are also dear friends), and to another two friends (Carrol Ross and Joyce Lindsay). They are my biggest supporters, and I thank them for their love, loyalty and faithfulness.

Thank-you,
Maxine Lantz

Other Books By This Author:

Rhyming Revelation
Flights Of Fancy
Covenant Of Care
Basking In The Son-Shine
Abundant Life

CONTENTS

A LETTER FROM YOUR BABY

You'll never see my smile, Mom, or see me play with toys.
You'll never hear my giggles for abortion was your choice.

You'll never walk me down the street on my first day of school.
You'll not have the opportunity to teach me the Golden Rule.

You'll never have the chance, Mom, to help when my heart breaks,
To advise me and to comfort. Abortion's the choice you made.

You'll never see me cross the stage on my graduation day,
Nor hear the cheers and the applause as I start my future way.

And when I wear the gown of white or watch my bride appear,
You'll never see my radiant smile or see my joyful tear.

You'll never hold my children on your lap and sing a song.
I hope you understand, Mom, the abortion choice was wrong.

But, Mom, know I forgive you. I'm in a happy place.
I'm held in Jesus' loving arms. I see His smiling face.

And, Mom, know God is willing to forgive you if you ask.
He'll restore your life and cleanse your heart, and in His love you'll bask.

So, Mom, please ask Him for forgiveness and, if you do, we'll spend
Eternity with Jesus. Our praises will not end.

ANGEL UNAWARE

I saw a man along the road,
A man unkempt, unclean .
His coat was dirty, torn and old-
The worst I'd ever seen.
He asked me for a bite to eat
As he shivered in the cold.
I gave the coat right off my back;
I had never been so bold.
We walked down to the diner
And I bought him a meal.
He asked me if I loved the Lord -
And if my love was real.
I told him, yes, I knew the Lord
I'd known him a few years.
I told him how Christ saved my life;
The old man shed a tear.
He gave me back my coat and said
That now he would be fine.
And though I urged he keep the coat
My offer was declined.
We parted and he walked away,
And I was taken by surprise,
For peeking out beneath his coat
I thought some wings I spied.
I shook my head; it could not be-
An angel? What's the odds
Of finding that this unkempt soul
Was an angel sent from God?
I know I'll never know for sure;
I know I'll never see
Was I an angel sent for him,
Or he an angel sent for me?

ANYONE, ANYTIME, ANYWHERE

A soul who bows the knee and claims Christ Jesus as its own
Will know the love of Jesus Christ and have all sins atoned.
A true repentant heart will find salvation in his Word
And it will see the faithfulness of Jesus Christ, the Lord.
Just come to Jesus and you'll find a love that knows no bounds
And God's own mercy, grace and love. Nowhere else can it be found!
There is no perfect time to near the cross at Calvary.
The moment when a heart repents is the moment it's set free.
One cannot say it's best at night, or when the sun is high.
I know the best time is the hour when to Calvary one draws nigh.
Just come to Jesus and confess you know that you have sinned
And Calvary's King will extend his arms and welcome you therein.
It need not be in a church or home, or a splendid palace tall.
The place where Christ is invited in does not matter to Him at all.
For He will take your gift of life that is marred and filled with sin,
And wash it in his red, red blood and make it new again.
Just come to Jesus, no matter where your heart calls out to His,
And Christ, in his great grace to you, will wash away your sins.
So, Friend, just know when you come to Christ, no import to the place.
You will feel the love of Jesus Christ, as He gently touches your face,
And says, "My child, I love you so. You now rest in my care,
My love is here for all to know. Anyone, anytime, anywhere.

ARMY OF BELIEF

Who can stand against God's people
If we march arm in arm?
With God as our commanding chief
We will never come to harm.

We must love one another
Each day and lend a hand
To build our brother and sister up.
With God, I know we can.

Satan will try to divide us
And cause us each to doubt
The love of God and others too,
But God will work it out.

So, let us march 'neath Jesus' flag
An army of belief
And rout the enemy each day
And give him no relief.

We'll fight the fight with armor on
And God's word as our sword.
We'll win each battle, every war,
If we'll just stand on God's own word.

And when the victory is secured
We'll stand and praise his name.
We'll tell others of our victory
That, through our God, we claim.

BORN OF GOD

"Yet to all who received him, to those who believed in his name, he gave the right to become children of God— children born not of natural descent, nor of human decision or a husband's will, but born of God."

John 1:12-13 NIV

I am born of God, and not of man,
Fulfilling God's salvation plan,
And as I daily this earth trod,
I know that I'm a child of God.

I reached a point where all I knew
Was what, in self, I could not do.
At that same hour, I knew the time
When Christ and all in Him was mine -

The peace that man can't comprehend,
The love, I know, that will not end,
The spring of joy within my heart,
The hope that Christ's harsh death imparts,

The mercy that I'm daily shown,
The grace that gave me sins atoned,
The talents that are mine to share
To show the world that Jesus cares.

Whatever happens here on earth,
I know that my soul's found its worth
Within God's great salvation plan
For I'm born of God, and not of man.

BOTHERED, BURDENED AND BLESSED

*Carry each other's burdens, and in this
way you will fulfill the law of Christ.*

Galatians 6:2 NIV

Father, make sure that I'm bothered
By the images I see.
Don't let me turn my eyes away
And be glad it isn't me.
The ragged clothes, the hungry eyes
Where no hope appears within.
To let me turn away from them
Would be a grievous sin.

Father, help me to be burdened
For all of the world's lost.
May I help in whatever way
But don't let me count the cost.
I know without the knowledge of
What Christ did on the cross,
These ones are damned to hell's hot fires
And will suffer heaven's loss.

Father, help me to bless others
I meet along life's path.
I'll use the gifts you've given me
To show your love will last,
To show how much you loved the world;
I can do nothing less.
And if I serve you, Father, then
I know I will be blessed.

I know your answer to this prayer
Will be in your own time.
Your holy will is what I ask
To overshadow mine.
And as I wait upon you, Lord,
And I rest in your care,
I pray with heartfelt gratitude
That you listen to my prayers.

CHRIST IN THEM, CHRIST IN ME

When Jesus came into my house
He wore no sparkling crown.
His dirty coat was ragged
And his shoes were well worn down.

When Jesus walked along my street
He wore no robes of white.
Because of layers of dirt and grime
His face was quite a sight.

When Jesus passed me by one day
He walked with an old cane.
His back was stooped and fingers gnarled.
Most looked on with disdain.

When Jesus came into the school
With hair all gelled and spiked,
Most people turned their face away
That "type" they did not like.

When Jesus "tagged" a local wall
With paint spray pink and green,
Most folks looked down at him with scorn
"Worst case I've ever seen".

But now I know the truth of life
The truth has set me free -
For if I don't see the Christ in them
They won't see the Christ in me.

COME, LIKE LITTLE CHILDREN

*Jesus said, "Let the little children come to
me, and do not hinder them, for the kingdom
of heaven belongs to such as these."*

Matthew 19:13-15 NIV

Come, like little children, who know how big God is.
Come, like little children, and know that you are His.
No thing's too small to ask of God; their faith puts us to shame.
They know the power and might of God and know to call His name.

Come, like little children, and walk up to the throne
Come, like little children, and his great love will be shown.
Just ask of God, expect results, and He will do the rest.
His answer, though it not be ours, will always be for best.

Come, like little children, and sit within his arms.
Come, like little children, and hide away from harm.
His arm of justice will prevail and sinners run and hide.
There is no earthly power that thrives when God is by our side.

Come, like little children, with faith as mustard seed
Come, like little children, in times of fear and need.
And God will listen to our prayers and give divine reply
If we, like little children, on His holy name will cry.

DID YOU HEAR WHAT THE ANGEL TOLD ME?

"But the angel said to her, "Do not be afraid, Mary, you have found favor with God. You will be with child and give birth to a son, and you are to give him the name Jesus. He will be great and will be called the Son of the Most High. The Lord God will give him the throne of his father David, and he will reign over the house of Jacob forever; his kingdom will never end."

Luke 1:30-33 NIV

Did you hear what the angel told me? Did you hear what the angel said?
When he first appeared on the pathway, my heart was filled with such dread.

But he told me not to be frightened. He told me to not be afraid.
He said by my Father in heaven that I was a favored maid.

He said I would become pregnant, but I just could not understand.
For you see I am a virgin and have never been with a man.

A son he said I would carry, and Jesus would be his new name.
But how will I ever tell Joseph? How will I ever explain?

Will Joseph turn and reject me? I wouldn't blame if he did!
But no matter the cost, I'll obey God and do what the Father has bid.

The Son of the Most High is what he will be, the angel then said to me.
He'll sit on his father David's throne, and no end to his reign will there be.

Each Israelite woman hoped she'd be the one to fulfill the old prophecy.
Yet God, in His grace, his mercy and love, showed favor and has chosen me.

Although I believe I'm unworthy to be the mother of God's only Son,
I'll do what the angel has told me, until my time here is done.

I know that my heart will be broken when I see God's salvation plan done,
But I know that throughout my time here on earth, I will shower love on his Son.

I'll love my sweet Jesus forever, and I'll always give him my best
Until my time is no longer and I enter God's eternal rest.

FORGIVEN BY GOD'S GRACE

The death warrant had been issued.
My name was on the line.
The punishment, I knew, was fair and just
For the crimes had all been mine.
My fate was sealed; no hope I had
That my life would not be gone.
I sorrowed for my choices made
And all that I had done.
But then a voice spoke in the court
"Release this one, I say".
I looked and there stood Jesus Christ,
The Truth, The Life, The Way.
"My child's repented of the sin
That brought upon this trial.
And I have washed his soul like new;
He's now pure and undefiled."
He took the warrant in His hand
And then wrote across its face
With nail-scarred hand that dripped in red,
"Forgiven by God's grace".

What joy then filled this new cleansed heart,
What peace was mine to know
As I recalled that Jesus Christ
On Calvary died to show
The love that is availed to all
Who with repentant hearts
Call out to Christ to save their souls
And a life with Him can start.
There's lots on earth to take my life,
But none can take my soul.
For Christ, in His resurrection hour,
Bought me and made me whole.

I am no longer of this earth
Though on this earth I trod.
For I am heaven's citizen
And a beloved child of God.
And when I slip this poor flawed earth
And look on Jesus' face,
I'll thank him for salvation's joy
And forgiveness by God's grace.

FRUIT OF THE SPIRIT

But the fruit of the Spirit is love, joy, peace,
patience, kindness, goodness, faithfulness,
gentleness and self-control.

Galatians 5:22 NIV

The Gardener plants the living seed that grows and bears much fruit.
Our lives will be the witness – the proof that God can do it.

A life transformed from selfish goals where what I want was king
To which He brought the gift of peace – His Holy Spirit within.

Because the Holy Spirit dwells within this soul unstained,
I know this vine will bear much fruit if, in Christ, I remain.

The fruit of love that ever shows the love of Christ, the King,
The fruit of joy that never leaves no matter what life brings.

The fruit of patience so we'll wait until Christ's time is revealed,
The fruit of kindness, goodness too, which to the world has great appeal,

The fruit of faithfulness we'll show to country, spouse and Lord
Will all be ours if we follow Christ and stay daily in His word.

And then the fruit of gentleness that Christ showed in His love
And self-control will come along with help from up above.

The vine the Gardener planted will wither and will die;
No fruit will grow upon its branch unless to God we cry

And beg him to fill up our soul with the Holy Spirit's aid,
Which then will let us show the world the change that God has made.

Then gentleness, joy and kindness, patience and self-control,
Faithfulness, goodness, peace and love will help us do our role

As children of the living God whose mission is to tell
The lost souls of this fallen world their destiny is hell.

But when they give their heart to Christ and on His name they call.
They'll share with God in glory – a hope available to all.

GIFTS AT THE CROSS

I stood beside the bloodstained cross
That stood on Calvary.
And Christ, through blood He shed that day
Bestowed these gifts on me:
His grace, unearned and freely given,
When on His name I called,
And yielded my repentant heart
To Christ – my all in all.
His love, so bountiful and great-
A love that has no end.
A love I know, without a doubt,
On which I can depend.
His mercy that sustains my life
With every breath I take.
Throughout each day, His mercy flows
From the moment I awake.
His forgiveness that, when I confess
My sin that caused Him grief,
Will cast the sin in ocean depths
And pardon I'll receive.
His holy Word, to lead and guide
Me in my daily walk.
And as I walk His narrow way,
I'll stand firm upon the Rock.
His power is availed to me,
His power and His might.
No earthly power compares to His,
In darkness or in light.
I stand beside the bloodstained cross
That stood on Calvary.
And thank Christ for the blood He shed
That bestowed these gifts on me.

GOD OF HOPE

*May the God of hope fill you with all joy and
peace as you trust in him so that you may overflow
with hope by the power of the Holy Spirit.*

Romans 15:13 NIV

God alone can grant the hope
That never seems to end.
From day to day, he'll give you hope.
On this you can depend.
The world of education
Cannot give that hope to you.
Philosophy and science
And theology can't, too.
There is no creed or tenet
That can light the darkest days
Except a faith in Jesus Christ.
The Truth, The Life, The Way.

When you have faith and know the power
Of Jesus and of God,
Your hope will overflow each day,
As on this earth you trod.
One cannot speak of all the joy
That wells within the heart.
Mere words cannot show the extent
Once our true believing starts,
And peace that we can't comprehend
Will fill our worried souls,
When we hand it over to the Lord
And He our troubles holds.

For trusting Christ, we can recall
The times and moments past,
When He was faithful and we know
That faithfulness will last.
And though we recall times ago,
We live in present times,
And our faith now will bring peace now,
And joy will come behind.
For without faith, we have no hope.
Without hope there is no peace.
And joy is lost without the love
Of God, which will not cease.

So here's the way that hope begins.
It's simple and it's sure.
Increasing faith will increase hope,
And peace and joy occur.
The Holy Spirit will give us power
To overflow with hope
When we are in dark days and nights,
We can begin to cope.
When others who can see our hope
Will question, we'll declare
"Our God's a God of hope, you see.
We're resting in his care."

GOD'S GRACE IN THE RACE

"However, I consider my life worth nothing to me, if only I may finish the race and complete the task the Lord Jesus has given me—the task of testifying to the gospel of God's grace."

Acts 20:24 NIV

My life's worth nothing if I can't finish the race,
Completing the task of testifying to grace.
The gospel of God's grace is what I can tell-
A life destined for heaven once destined for hell.
The race won't be easy, but I know that He's there
To keep me from falling, for I know that He cares.
Throughout all life's circumstance, I'm held in his hand.
No matter what happens, He will help me to stand.
His grace I can't borrow, can't barter or buy;
It's freely dispensed from the God throne on high.
God's grace has no limits, no borders, no end –
Just a holy supply on which I can depend.
And when, in the race, I may stumble and fall
God's grace picks me up and I again can stand tall,
Secure that my falter will not be the cause
Of losing the grace that I have now from God.
So I will run onward 'til the end line's in sight,
Empowered by God's love, his mercy and might.
And when, at the last, when the line has been crossed,
When life is no longer, and strivings are lost,
My hope now is that I will hear my God say,
"You've run the race well, Child. You're now home to stay."

HELP ME TO REMEMBER

"Here is a boy with five small barley loaves and two small fish, but how far will they go among so many?"

When life presents circumstance
That I think I can't bear,
Help me to remember
That I rest in your care.
When doubt enters my mind,
And I don't look to you,
Help me to remember
All the things you can do.
When trials and temptations
Take over my place,
Help me to remember
I'm within reach of your grace.
And when I'm down at the bottom
And the only way's up,
Help me to remember
Just how full is my cup.
And, Lord, when I stumble,
Help me understand
That I won't ever falter,
For I'm held in your hand.
Help me to remember
That your love has no end,
That forever I know
I can trust and depend
That your grace and mercy
Will be there when I call.
That brings peace to my soul, Lord,
You're my all in all!

HE'S WITH YOU

He's with you on the mountain top
Or on the valley floor.
He paid the price on Calvary's cross
To open heaven's door.

And when you think you're all alone
And there's no one left to care,
Then know the reason why He died
Was a love so strong, so rare.

His great love knows no limits,
Mercy and grace as well.
He showed it when He bore the cross
To save mankind from hell.

Just know that when you yield your heart
And lay it at Christ's feet,
You'll know his love and mercy too,
And your joy will be complete.

For when you know that Jesus died
To save us from our sin,
The peace that man can't comprehend
Will fill your soul within.

And you can say without a doubt
And know that this is true,
In Christ's great love, there is no fear
For He'll always walk with you.

I AM A MIGHTY GOD

*"if my people, who are called by my name, will humble
themselves and pray and seek my face and turn from
their wicked ways, then will I hear from heaven and
will forgive their sin and will heal their land."*

2 Chronicles 7:14 NIV

I am a mighty God and there is no great might like mine.
My breath created all the earth; salvation's my design.
My people, whom I've chosen, are called now by my name
And if they walk my narrow way, they'll never suffer shame.
But if they turn away from me and live their wicked ways,
Then they will never see my face throughout their evil days.
But, if they pray to me, their God, in true humility
Then I will hear from heaven and my power they will see.
Their sins will be forgiven and they'll walk again in light.
They'll be a restored people for they're precious in my sight.
Their lives will have abundance of my mercy, love and grace.
They'll rest forever so secure in their Father's sweet embrace.
And then, when they've repented and with me again they stand,
Then I will stretch out my right hand, and I will heal their land.

I AM A PRAYER WARRIOR

I am a prayer warrior.
I spend my day in prayer.
I know the Lord is able
To handle me with care.
He lets me know He loves me
And knows I love Him too.
I only have to ask Him;
He'll show me what to do.

I know that there are others
Who say He isn't here,
And yet they don't persuade me –
My answer's always clear.
Although I cannot see Him,
In Him I put my faith.
He knows me like a father,
And always shows the way.

Whenever I have trials,
And sorrows come around,
He always shows His presence
And blessings e'er abound.
He puts His arms around me
Ad whispers, meek and mild,
"I'll always be here with you.
I love you, my dear child."

I AM PREPARED TO GO

I do not know the hour or day
When you will call me home.
I do not know if day or night,
But I'm prepared to go.

I have the quiet assurance
I'll share eternity
With Christ, my Lord and Savior
Who shed His blood for me.

Anticipation fills my heart
When I think of that day
When you will say, "Come home, my child."
And I will soar away.

What joy will fill my ransomed heart
When I look on your face
And see the thorn marks on your brow;
You bore them in my place.

I'll see your nail-scarred hands and feet,
Your sword-pierced side as well.
In grateful adoration, Lord,
Your praises will I tell.

Because you showed such love to me,
I hope the world knows
That, though I know not hour or day,
I am prepared to go.

I KNOW THAT MY REDEEMER LIVES!

*"I know that my Redeemer lives, and that in
the end he will stand upon the earth."*

Job 19:25 NIV

I know that my Redeemer lives,
No matter what is said.
The world says he never was
Or says that Christ is dead.
But in my heart, I know the truth
That Jesus rose again
And stole the victory from the grave
To cancel man's heart stain.
He could have whispered it to be
Or shouted from the hills;
Instead he chose to live on earth
And obey his Father's will.
He chose to die upon the cross
In torturous pain and shame.
When he hung there upon the tree
He knew my sin and name.
He knew without his sacrifice
My soul was bound for hell;
I could not enter heaven.
These facts he knew full well.
I also know because he rose
He reigns with God above,
To intercede with God for me
In wisdom and in love.
I know he'll stand upon the earth
In dominion o'er the world;
Every knee will bow and tongue confess
That Jesus Christ is Lord.
While I am living on this earth
Great praises I will give
For Christ, who saved me from my sin.
My great Redeemer lives!

I LAY MY LIFE WITHIN YOUR HAND

I lay my life within your hand;
I know its fate's secure
For naught can pluck me from your hand.
This fact I know for sure.

Don't let me take it back again
And try to go my way.
I know the power resides in you
So in your hand I'll stay.

I know that everything I need
For now and evermore
Is found in your unfailing love
And heaven's richest store.

Your grace bestowed in time of need,
Your love that knows no end,
Your mercy shown to me always,
On these I can depend.

So, Lord, please let me rest secure
Within your holy hand
Until my soul slips this flawed earth
And joins the heavenly band.

I MAY NOT KNOW

I may not know how high's the moon
Or where the wind takes rest.
But this I know without a doubt,
Your love for me's the best.

I may not know a tiger's ways
Or the mind set of a flea.
But this I know without a doubt
Your love's the best for me.

I may not know why bubbles float
Or how a giggle starts.
But this I know without a doubt
Your love is in my heart.

I may not know why sheep go "baa"
Or pigeons bill and coo.
But this I know without a doubt
Your love is steadfast, true.

I may not know why little ants
Can carry times their weight.
But this I know without a doubt
Your love for me is great.

There are many things I do not know
I'll admit; it's true indeed.
But this I know for all my years
Your love is all I need.

IN LOVE

In love you bore that heavy cross
Right up to Calvary's place.
Your precious back was scourged and torn
And blood ran down your face.
There was no moment when you thought
To call your angels down.
Instead you thought of me, Dear Lord,
And wore their thorny crown.

In love, you let them nail you there
To that old, cruel rugged cross
So that my sins could be erased
And you didn't count the cost.
In all your silent suffering,
Amidst the scorn and hate-filled words,
Your love spoke volumes to the crowd,
But they didn't listen, Lord.

In love, you suffered cruel death
By hanging on that tree
And even if I'd been just one,
You'd still have died for me.
In love, you rose in your great power
My sin-stained soul to save.
You broke death's hold on me that day
And stole victory from the grave.

In love, you rose to heaven's door
And sit at God's right hand.
To bridge the gap 'tween God and me
And intercede for man.
So, we that know you as our King,
Our Advocate above,
All know that when you saved our souls
You did it out of love.

In love, I thank you for the hope
That one day by and by,
I'll join the saints in glorious throng
And this will be my cry,
"I was loved by God before my birth.
I was loved by God each day.
I'll be loved by Him forevermore
As we walk the golden way."

IN THE HOLLOW OF HIS HAND

I do not know the mind of God
But I still rest in His will.
And when the world gets out of sorts,
I can stay there, quiet and still.

There is a comfort in that place,
The hollow of His hand,
That the world will never ever know
But believers understand.

When days are good, I stand up tall
And shout for all to hear
That my God is a mighty God.
I can stand up without fear.

But when some trials come around,
And my world seems less secure,
I can rest in His protection
For I know His power endures.

He lets me stay within His hand,
And peek out at the foe.
I can rest assured He'll stay with me
For He said He'll never go.

And when the giants come around
He lets me sit against His hand
And look away from those huge giants.
'Til by His grace, I'll once more stand.

Together, we will conquer
The evil giants in my world.
And once again I'll stand upright
And shout the glories of my Lord.

IN THE RUINS

"Just as I watched over them to uproot and tear down, and to overthrow, destroy and bring disaster, so I will watch over them to build and to plant," declared the LORD.

Jeremiah 31:28

I'm sitting in the rubble, Lord;
My whole life is in ruins.
I don't know how it happened, Lord.
I don't know what you're doing.
I know that I cannot rebuild
For my feeble strength's now done.
And yet I know my weakness will
Be turned to strength in Christ, your son.
So help me to pick up each piece,
According to your master plan,
And place it on the other bricks
Assured I'm resting in your hands.
And while I'm placing brick on brick,
Help me to stop and then reflect
On why you brought such ruin on me.
Is it choices made? Is it a test?
If choices made caused this result,
I ask forgiveness for each time
I placed your will far from my life
And gave the prominence to mine.
And if the ruins are a test,
Help me to live (it's my desire)
Assured that you will never leave
My side as I walk through the fire.
I'll thank you, Lord, when we pass through,
And praise you for your grace and love,
Content I placed each brick in place
As part of God's great plan above.

I WILL SEEK YOU

I will seek you in the morning
When the day has just begun.
I will gaze on your creation
And be amazed by what you've done.
I will pray that you'll walk with me,
That my thoughts will be on you
When I seek you in the morning,
When the day is fresh and new.

I will seek you, Lord, at mid-day
When my day is half-way through.
I'll look back at your provision
Of blessings for me from you.
I will pray the world won't win, Lord,
As I spend each passing hour,
And I know that I will be availed
Of your might and of your power.

I will seek you, Lord, at night-time
When the daylight fades and dies.
I will thank you for your faithfulness
As you tarried by my side.
I will thank you for your love, Lord,
On which I ever can depend.
And I'll seek you, Lord, at night-time
When the day has found an end.

LINE OF GRACE

There is a line of grace that's drawn
Between the worlds of right and wrong.
And those who live on evil's side
In lives of darkness all reside.
While those who live on side of right
Know Jesus' love and His great might.
Each one once lived on side of wrong
And to the darkened world belonged.
But they, the hour when they first called
On Jesus' name, received it all -
His mercy, grace and His great love
Bestowed on them from up above.
If some would choose to cross that line,
From sin-stained world to life divine,
Their hearts must repent of their sin
And let Christ Jesus enter in.
What joy! What rapture will occur
When their salvation is ensured.
I too once lived on darkened side
And knew, as lord, my self and pride.
But on that day, when Christ came in
I yielded up my life of sin.
What I gave up had not a cost
For I gained life at Calvary's cross.
I now know Christ as Lord and King,
And in Him I can do all things.
As He forgave, I'll do the same
And do it all in Jesus' name.
The day I see Him, face-to-face,
I'll thank Him for that line of grace.

LOOKING AHEAD

Oh, what a wondrous thought I see –
My living with Christ for eternity,
My praising His name at the throne of grace,
And looking into my Savior's face.

Oh, what a wondrous thought I see –
My living with Christ for eternity,
My sharing all time with beloved saints
With no time or distance as my constraints.

Oh, what a wondrous thought I see –
My living with Christ for eternity,
My telling the angels what God has done
That by His grace, I had sins atoned.

Oh, what a wondrous thought I see –
My living with Christ for eternity,
My seeing for real what I now only believe
And my Savior's side I will never leave.

LORD, HELP ME TO REMEMBER

When dark clouds billow over me
And the moon cannot be seen,
Then, Lord, help me to remember
The places that we've been.

I've stood atop the mountain
And breathed the cool, fresh air.
I did not stand there by myself
For you were always there.

I was low down in the valley
When I could barely stand.
I may have stumbled, but never fell,
For I was held by your dear hand.

So, Lord, help me to remember
What you have clearly shown -
That no matter what the circumstance
I have never walked alone.

LORD OF HEAVEN AND EARTH

"The God who made the world and everything in it is the
Lord of heaven and earth and does not live in temples
built by hands. And he is not served by human hands, as
if he needed anything, because he himself gives all men
life and breath and everything else. From one man he
made every nation of men, that they should inhabit the
whole earth; and he determined the times set for them and
the exact places where they should live. God did this so
that men would seek him and perhaps reach out for him
and find him, though he is not far from each one of us.

Acts 17:24-27 NIV

The very God who made the world
And all that it contains
Sits up on high in glory and
In righteousness He reigns.

He does not live in temples built
By the work of human hands.
He does not need a single thing
For He owns all the lands.

He is not served by human hands
For it's He that gives us breath.
His mercies daily to us shown
Are each day created fresh.

From one man He created
All nations so that they
Should earth inhabit, in God's plan,
And follow in God's way.

He set out times for all of them
And picked where they would be
So that they would reach out for Him
And find the way to liberty.

No one would have to search too far
For God is ever near.
He'll join us in our victory times
Or hold us when we fear.

We are His offspring, it is said,
The children of His heart.
In Him, we'll find a peace and joy
That He'll, to us, impart.

LOVE, JOY, PEACE

Love was found in a manger, warmed by the breath of the beasts.
Shepherds heard the angels and wise men came from the east.

Who knew this babe would save us? Who knew the Father's plan
That sent his only precious Son to save earth's sin-stained man?

Such **love** I cannot understand; such **love** my soul astounds.
God's **love** was shown that Christmas morn
when **Love** in a manger was found.

♥ ♥ ♥ ♥ ♥ ♥ ♥

The earth says **joy** is fleeting and on circumstance depends,
But **joy** from Christ will ever last - a **joy** that has no end.

Joy from Christ will overcome all distance, time and place
For true **joy** comes from knowing Him – His mercy, love and grace.

So live with **joy**, and serve with **joy**. Let your **joy** well overflow.
For Christ, who was born that Christmas morn,
is the source of the **joy** you know.

∪ ∪ ∪ ∪ ∪ ∪ ∪

Peace does not mean without danger, but the presence of God's only Son.
And **peace** can be found in knowing Him well
- the Alpha and Omega! The One!

The world can never comprehend the source of such great **peace**!
We know it is our Savior, Christ, for his care and love won't cease.

We sit within the Father's hand, and nothing can cause us to fall.
The gift of **peace** was given to us when on Christ's name we called.

∨ ∨ ∨ ∨ ∨ ∨ ∨

So the gifts we got that Christmas morn were precious beyond compare.
For Christ, the greatest gift received, was born in that stable, cold and bare.

A child who'd one day bear my sins and die on Calvary's cross
To cleanse my soul and set me free, so heaven won't be lost.

God's gift of love without an end, the gift of peace and joy
Were wrapped in swaddling clothes that day, Mary's precious baby boy.

MARY'S CHRISTMAS STORY

Once upon a long time, in a land far, far away
I, Mary, laid my new-born son upon a bed of hay.
I counted all his fingers. I counted all his toes.
I marveled at the beauty of his eyes, ears, mouth and nose.

I wrapped swaddling clothes around him to keep him from the cold.
I loved him. Oh, how I loved him. And I remembered I'd been told
That I would be the mother of the Savior of the earth,
That my baby boy would one day grow and give all mankind worth.

The angel then had told me that Jesus was his name.
I knew that with his coming, the world would never be the same.
And as I watched him sleeping, with a smile upon his face,
I marveled at the gift I had – all given through God's grace.

The shepherds came and told a tale, that an angel had appeared.
They were terrified, but the angel said "There's no reason for your fear.
Today in Bethlehem's blessed town, the Christ-child has been born.
You'll find him wrapped in swaddling clothes in a manger, so forlorn."

Then a heavenly choir of angels had appeared in night's dark sky,
Singing praises and saying "Peace on earth and all glory to God on high".
The shepherds then decided to visit Bethlehem's town.
The found the Babe in the manger, all wrapped in swaddling gown.

Showing adoration to the Christ, they knelt on bended knee,
Then ran and told all whom they met of what they'd heard and seen-
Of the angels singing in the sky, of the Christ-child's lowly birth,
Of the Savior who had come to save all the lost souls here on earth.

I rose to meet the Wise Men as they came on camels' backs.
I wondered what they searched for as they rummaged in their packs.
They knelt before my baby, 'neath the brightly shining star,
And told a tale of journey from a country very far.

They opened up their presents, and it made perfect sense
To present them to my baby boy – gold, myrrh and frankincense.
They talked about a visit to a king – Herod, by name –
Who wished to come and worship Christ; at least that's what he claimed.

But do not worry, dear friends. I ask you not to fear
For to the Wise Men, in a dream, God's angel did appear
And told the Wise Men Herod wished to kill the child, not pray.
So when the Wise Men traveled home, they went another way.

So, Dear Friends, on this Christmas Day, I ask you just these things:
Remember the Babe of Bethlehem, remember Christ the King.
Remember that He loves you, remember always to say:
"I love you, dearest Jesus, and I'll walk your narrow way."

MESSIAH IN A MANGER

My Lord lay in a manger where cattle came to feed -
A truly holy Savior who came to intercede.
He did not come in as a king, with armies all around,
But in a lowly stable is where my King was found.
He came to earth in human form, and lay on humble hay,
And Mary stored up in her heart what the angel had to say.
She knew her son had come to earth to save all man from sin;
She knew her son would have to die to make men clean again.
And Joseph stood right by her side, and there recalled his dream
When he was told by angels that this child would man redeem.
They looked upon that little boy, and vowed to do their best
To love him and to help him grow until he met his test.
That test would have him saying, "Father, if it's thy will,
Then take this cup of sorrows and I won't climb that hill.
I'll not be beaten, shamed and scorned. My name they'll not deride.
But I now accept whatever end your holy will decides.
For, Father, let it be thy way; my will takes second place.
On cruel cross I'll yield my life to gain salvation's grace
For sinful man whose heart repents and calls with desperate plea,
And sin-dark souls will be made clean by my blood at Calvary."
Their hearts knew what lay far ahead, but on that Christmas morn
They only thought of this new life, and thanked God that he was born.
Their hearts were full of love that day as Christ, the God-Child lay
So helpless in his human form, upon that humble hay.
And then the shepherds came and told of angel choirs at night,
Proclaiming news – Messiah's birth – and glory shining bright.
The wise men came and brought him gifts, and told of shining star
That they had followed many days from homes in lands afar.
Some frankincense was offered, some myrrh and precious gold-
Such gifts of worth presented to the Messiah long foretold.
We, too, can bring a gift to Him whose death on Calvary's cross
Ensured for those who will believe they won't suffer heaven's loss.

Our gifts don't need a package, with a bow so neatly tied
For all we need to gain such prize is on Jesus' name to cry
And admit that we are sinners in need of saving grace.
All doubt and fear will be swept away, and peace will take their place.
We'll give up dross that filled our lives before we saw the light
And gain love, peace and mercy and know heaven is in sight.
So when you think of that Christmas morn that happened long ago,
When Jesus came as a helpless babe, God's redemption plan to show,
Then thank God for salvation, through Christ's death on Calvary,
That started in a manger where cattle came to feed.

MIRACLE OF MIRACLES

The tomb claimed Lazarus as its own; he no longer walked this earth.
Then Jesus gave his great command, "Dear Lazarus, come forth".
And Lazarus rose, with shroud-clad head, and from the tomb came out.
It was his resurrection hour – a true miracle, no doubt.
All those who saw that miracle could not believe their eyes –
That Lazarus stood in front of them when they had seen him die.

The demons had possessed the man and none could hold him down.
They burned and harmed their human host as he roamed throughout the town.
But the demons recognized the Lord and pled that he'd relent.
And so, into a herd of pigs, the devils were all sent.
The man was saved from Satan's snares; his mind was all restored.
But the people asked the Lord to leave and to return no more.

The man, who had been blind from birth, was begging at the gate.
When Jesus passed him by, he knew that Christ could change his fate.
Christ made a paste of spit and mud and placed it on his eyes,
Told him to wash in Siloam's Pool; he obeyed and gained his sight.
And all who'd known the man from birth, and knew his sightless past,
All marveled at the miracle that, that day, had come to pass.

The woman bled for twelve long years; her life a living hell.
She knew that Christ, and Christ alone, could somehow make her well.
She pressed against the throng that day, and finally touched his cloak.
He knew His power had been released, and then the Master spoke.
The woman, frightened and ashamed, began her tale of woe.
But Jesus said, "Your faith is much. Be healed. Now you may go."

The master of the wedding feast had run out of the wine.
And when his mother asked him to, Christ performed a feat divine.
They poured the water into jars and then on Christ's command,
They placed a cup of finest wine into the wedding master's hand.
He did not know the miracle it took to make that change,
But those that saw Christ's mighty power would never be the same.

The crowds had come to hear Christ speak, but food was very scarce.
The disciples knew they had no food to feed the thousands there.
They only had two tiny fish and they had five loaves of bread.
But with God's blessing on the food, five thousand folks were fed.
And when the crumbs were gathered up, the baskets numbered twelve.
Another miracle performed - Christ's might and power to tell.

There's yet another miracle that's not found within God's word.
The miracle took place the day I surrendered to the Lord.
And a soul, dark-stained with sin and shame, took on a brand new hue.
The whiteness of my cleansed soul showed God's great love, ever true.
I know the joy and peace of Christ; all his goodness I recall
When I think again of rescued soul – the greatest miracle of all.

MOURNING INTO DANCING

"You turned my wailing into dancing; you removed
my sackcloth and clothed me with joy, that my
heart may sing to you and not be silent. O LORD
my God, I will give you thanks forever."

Psalm 30:11-12 NIV

Where once I saw the thorns and briers,
Now bloom the flowers fair.
Where once the world seemed cold and dark
I now see sunshine there.
Where once I walked with downcast head,
I now raise it to the sky.
Where once I thought my life was o'er,
I now have dreams to try.
I did not make this change alone;
You walked right by my side.
Instead of wailing, now I dance,
The Bridegroom with his bride.
You took my sackcloth and you gave me
Clothes of joy and peace.
My heart cannot stay silent, Lord;
My praise can't ever cease.

MY CAPTAIN, LORD AND KING

When winds of life my ship assail,
My Captain will, I know, not fail
To keep it steady through the gale.
My Captain, Lord and King.

Though Satan lays his traps and snares,
And tries to catch me unawares,
I rest within the loving care
Of my Captain, Lord and King.

When circumstances make me fear,
I just remember that He's near,
And that he'll make my pathway clear.
My Captain, Lord and King.

And when I sail life's seas no more,
And I, with joy, reach heaven's door,
I know my praises will be for
My Captain, Lord and King.

MY GIFT AT THE CROSS

I walked up to the Savior's cross
And laid my present there.
The wrappings were not beautiful;
No bows did that gift wear.
Inside were all my fears and doubts,
My past with all my sins.
Would He accept what I had brought
And let this sinner in?

I watched and waited. Then I saw
Christ reach down from the cross.
He took the present in His hands,
Took no mind of the dross.
I held my breath in dread and fear
That He'd cast it away.
"Please, Lord, accept me for your child"
Were all the words I prayed.

Then, I could not believe my eyes
For as I stood and stared,
The present that I'd given Him
Began to glow, so fair.
The wrapping gleamed a holy light,
A bow appeared on top.
Christ had my gift accepted there.
My tears could not be stopped.

To my surprise, Christ handed me
A gift with His own hands.
The wrappings were of many hues.
I did not understand.
I opened up the box He gave
And took a look inside.
And there lay peace, and joy and love
That in my heart will e'er abide.

MY GOD

Give thanks to the LORD and call on his name.
For what he has done he is due our acclaim.
Tell all of the nations and his name exalt.
Our praises and worship shouldn't come to a halt.

His power is mighty; his judgments are just.
In this God alone I deposit my trust.
With my God beside me, I can do all things.
He is an awesome, amazing King!

Our words cannot fully give thanks for His grace.
Our actions should honor as we run the race.
The world should be able to see we belong
To God, who is able to keep us from wrong.

No earthly idol with mute mouth can compare.
No carved earthly image is able to care
For all of the details of our earthly lives
As we, in our weakness, continue to strive.

No mere god can give us the joy and the peace
And love, without limits, that will never cease.
They can't give assurance of what we will gain
When death claims our body and the spirit remains.

I know that peace, joy and love my God shows.
He is constantly with me wherever I go.
My soul will wing skyward when death claims this shell
Assured of salvation that saved me from hell.

I'll keep singing praises as I bow 'fore His throne,
In grateful thanksgiving for the love He has shown.
Throughout all the ages, my song will remain
Hosanna! Hosanna! Bless God's holy name.

MY LORD IS FAITHFUL

Lord, when my heart's in deep despair,
Help me recall you're always there.
When all around is deep and dark,
Help me your voice to heed and hark.
When life's cruel trials steal all hope,
I'll hold your hand; you'll help me cope.
When my heart soars with joy so rare,
I'll dance within your loving care.
When all the world is shining bright,
Your love will be what chased the night.
When I am filled with hope profound,
No fear in tribulation found,
Then I can say, "In trials grim,
My Lord was faithful; I trust Him.
No matter what the time or day,
My Savior walked with me each day.
On mountain peak or valley floor,
I'll love my God forevermore."

MY PRAYER

"Oh, that you would bless me and enlarge my territory! Let your hand be with me, and keep me from harm so that I will be free from pain."

1 Chronicles 9:4 NIV

Father, that you would bless me
And not limit where I go
To tell to all the nations
Just how you love them so.
Please let your hand be on me,
And keep me from all harm.
May your love surround completely,
And keep me safe and warm.
May you comfort me in sorrow,
And in times of cruel pain.
May I see your loving hand of grace,
Time and time again.
And we'll dance in times of triumph
And sing victory's great song.
I know that in each circumstance
I'm assured you walk along.
And may your Spirit help me show
To all the world's lost,
The mighty power that's in your name.
Help me not to count the cost.
May nothing ever come before,
Neither family nor friend.
May I never in my own power rest
And on yours ever depend.
May my assurance of my home
That's not here on this earth
Impel me on to works for you,
Where my soul will find its worth.

MY REDEEMER LIVES!

*I know that my Redeemer lives, and that in
the end he will stand upon the earth."*

Job 19:25 NIV

There is a wondrous fact to tell;
My heart knows that it's true.
I know that my Redeemer lives
And know what He can do.

Although the world scorns His name
And tries to shut Him out,
There is no power on earth that can;
He is God, without a doubt.

The world supposed that, on His death,
His might would be no more.
But, in that resurrection hour,
He opened heaven's door.

And all that call upon His name
With a true repentant heart,
Will gain His mercy and His grace
And a Friend who won't depart.

They'll gain a love beyond degree,
A love that knows no bounds,
And grace bestowed and mercy too.
These all in Christ are found.

And yet, another wonder waits,
A wonder of great worth.
That Christ, the great Redeemer Lord,
Will stand upon the earth.

He'll stand upon the earth that He,
With one word, brought to be,
And people of all nations then,
His power and might will see.

All knees will bow; all tongues confess
That Christ is Lord and King.
And those that scorned will go to hell
But believers Christ will bring

To share eternity with Him
And God, the Father, too.
All this I've told you will occur;
The facts are right and true.

One last thought that I have is this
(Such comfort this thought gives)
That I walk with sins atoned and cleansed
For my Redeemer lives!

MY REFUGE AND ROCK

Written after reading Psalm 18

I love you, O Lord. You're my strength and my rock,
My refuge in whom I can hide.
My stronghold, my shield, when I call on you, Lord,
You are with me, right close to my side.

You are worthy of praise; you defeated my foes
When the death cords entangled and snared.
Then in my deep distress, I cried out to you, Lord,
In your throne room, you heard my despair.

The earth trembled and shook, and your fierce wrath was shown
In the thunder, and lightning and hail.
Then you reached from on high and took hold of my hand
And my foes had no chance to prevail.

For although they were strong, and alone I was weak,
With you, Lord, I know victory's assured.
For you said you will stay by my side every day.
I've your promise in your Holy word.

MY SON

Hello, my son. You're finally here.
We've waited for so long.
I know the angel told your fate,
But I'm hoping he was wrong.
You seem so little in my arms;
Your beauty takes my breath.
How could the angel say that you
Would die a grievous death?

Good day, my son. My how you've grown!
Your babyhood is gone.
You're helping Joseph in his shop;
You're growing tall and strong.
You're not a babe, not quite a man,
You're somewhere in between.
I'm storing up my memories
For the angel-foretold scene.

Good work, my son. I see the way
Your ministry is going.
I see you doing your Father's will
And God's love to all are showing.
I know it will not be too long
Until your time comes due
To die on Calvary, as was told.
My heart near breaks in two!

My dear, dear son, I cannot see
Your form upon the cross,
For tears are flowing from my eyes
At my impending loss.
I'll miss you, Son, but I do know
That you'll fulfill God's will.
My heart is breaking for you, Son,
As I see you hanging still.

Good bye, my son. We'll meet again
For you told me that is so.
I know you'll lie within the tomb
For three days, and the foe
Will think he's seen the last of you,
And that he has all power.
You'll break his power of death and grave
In your resurrection hour.

Hello, my Son. I'm here at last.
I've waited for so long.
I know you sit at God's right hand;
It's the place where you belong.
I see the face I've missed for years;
I see the nail-pierced scars.
I see the prints of thorny crown
That your holy beauty marred.

My son, a mother's love won't dim
Or vanish in a breath.
I've loved you from the very first,
And long after your death.
I lived my life with just one hope-
To see you once again.
And now I'll live eternally
With you and all the saints.

O SHEPHERD, DEAR SHEPHERD

*If a man owns a hundred sheep, and one of them wanders
away, will he not leave the ninety-nine on the hills and
go to look for the one that wandered off? And if he finds
it, I tell you the truth, he is happier about that one sheep
than about the ninety-nine that did not wander off.*

Matthew 18: 12-13

O Shepherd, Dear Shepherd,
I'm lost and I fear.
I'm cold and I'm lonely
And wolves howl near.

The night's getting darker
And clouds hide the moon.
O Shepherd, Dear Shepherd,
Please come find me soon.

You said if I ever
Strayed far and got lost
That you'd come and find me,
No matter the cost.

You'd leave all the others
And come looking for me,
And when, Shepherd, you found me
Your deep joy I'd see.

I'd stay in your presence
And not leave your side.
In your love and your mercy
I'd ever abide.

PLEASE, GOD

In times of trouble, help me see
That you, my God, are all I need.
And when I look for man's applause
Please pull me back and help me pause
To recall all that you have done –
You gave me life through your own son.
On me you have bestowed your grace
And in your kingdom special place
As heir with Jesus Christ, my Lord.
What else compares within this world?

In times of doubt, please let me stay
Upon the path of the only way.
Don't let the world push me aside.
Help me, with faith, in you abide.
Don't let my fears erase my faith
As I walk this earth from day to day.
And should I meet a man dread-filled
Then let me stay in your holy will
And tell that man if he should ask,
"My God can always do the task."

No matter what life's circumstance
Doubt and fear won't stand a chance
For deep within my heart, I know
Your love for me you'll always show.
Your mercy and your grace is mine;
All given by your hand divine.
Your love is unconditional, too,
My life, my all, I give to you.
For without you, my life would end.
I know on you, Lord, I can depend.

POPPIES ON A CROSS

White crosses lined up in a row
The love of fellow man to show.
The air is calm; some sounds are heard-
The force of wind and whistling birds;
The scenes of war cannot compare
With sounds of death and dieing there.
The stones though covered all in moss
Still show us poppies on the cross.

White crosses lined up in a row
The love of fellow man to show.
Each grave a haven for the dreams,
The full potential and the schemes
Of the brave soldier buried there.
Each mourning family had to bear
The searing pain and sense of loss
Portrayed by poppies on a cross.

White crosses lined up in a row
The love of fellow man to show.
The soldiers did not count the price
When yielding life in sacrifice.
They loved their country and believed
Their sacrifice would bring us peace.
They knew their death could be the cost
Of poppies anchored to a cross.

White crosses lined up in a row
The love of fellow man to show
Demands that we remember they
Who yielded up their lives to pay
The price of freedom - paid in red
By those who lived but now are dead.
They all believed in freedom's cause
And we see poppies on a cross.

PURSUED UNTIL PARDONED

I ran from God so unaware of what I'd miss within his care.
I did not know what treasures vast were lost to me as I ran fast.
And Satan ran along beside and told me all his vicious lies.
He said I had no need of Christ, that in myself the power lied.
That I would be all that I could if I, within my own power, stood.
My power, he said, was deep within. He never mentioned once my sin.
But God was with me as I ran and one day, in His sovereign plan,
He put a saint upon my path who told me of God's love that lasts.
He told me of my sin-dark state, and of my need to make things straight
With Christ, who died on Calvary's tree for sinners stained with sin, like me.
He spoke of life, cleansed and renewed, of life eternal. Then I knew
That Christ was what I needed most. And now, in His great love, I boast
Of joy and peace repentance brought. Through Christ's shed blood, I now am bought-
A bond slave of my Christ, and King who now, to me, is everything.
And through my time on earth, I'll tell how I gained heaven and escaped hell,
How Satan's lies were proved all wrong. I now to Christ, my King, belong.
And I will thank for gifts, all free, His love, His grace, and liberty
From Satan's plots to win my soul, and make me fear and keep control.
Thank God, who made salvation's plan and Christ who followed me as I ran.

RESURRECTION DAY

The rulers thought they'd won the game –
The tomb was closed and sealed.
They were not there, and did not see,
God's awesome power revealed.

For Christ, who'd died just days before,
Arose in might and power
And stole the victory from Death.
What a truly glorious hour!

For none before and none to come
Will rise from death's cold chains
To sit in glory at God's right hand
And leave the death clothes where they lay.

And through Christ's death upon the cross
And the Resurrection Day
All sinners who repent and walk
In God's holy and righteous way

Will gain eternal life, and more,
Will see God face to face
And thank the Lamb of God who took
Each sin-stained sinner's place.

ROOTS OF FAITH

May I rest by living water
That gives abundant life so free.
May everything around me
Remind me, Lord, of Thee.

When woe and strife surround me,
When I'm in my darkest hour
Then, Lord, let me sink my roots deep
Into your awesome power.

Let me draw, Lord, from your mercy,
Your great grace and your love.
Let me know the deep abiding peace
That only comes from up above.

For if I try to overcome
On my feeble power alone,
My plan will not be fruitful,
And my weaknesses are shown.

But in my daily walk I know
That you are always near.
Though wind and drought are present
Lord, I know I've naught to fear.

For my faith roots go much deeper
Than the circumstance I see,
And I'll stand upright, unscathed and strong,
For I know you walk with me.

SERVANT, SACRIFICE, SUBSTITUTE

You chose to serve man, at great cost,
And came to earth to Calvary's cross.
A lowly manger held your birth
The day that you arrived on earth.
No trumpets sounded to proclaim
A king was born the day you came.
Your life on earth was not of ease,
And yet to heaven you held the keys.
You gifted sight to blinded eyes
And told the world of Satan's lies.
You raised the dead, and in God's name,
You fed five thousand, healed the lame.
What sacrifice did Calvary see
That gave my soul its liberty?
They spat on you and your name scorned
And made you wear a crown of thorns.
They nailed you to that cruel tree
And raised you up so all could see.
They scourged your back, and pierced your side
And did your holy name deride.
They mocked you when they called you king
And yet no condemnation did you bring.
You brought salvation at such a price –
Your holy, willing sacrifice.
I should have hung there on that tree
And yet you took my place for me.
I should have been there on that cross
And yet you saved my soul from loss.
The scourging all belonged to me,
The searing pain and agony.
I should have borne the guilt and shame,
And heard the crowd deride my name.
But, in the love you had for me,
You hung there on that cruel tree.
You showed a love that's so acute.
You are my King and Substitute!

TAKE UP MY CROSS

If anyone would follow me, then this he must know well,
That daily he must take my cross and must deny himself.
Each day will bring a chance to bear my cross for my name's sake
But also each new day will bring a time of choice to make.
If he will count his life worth more than my cross, then I'll know
That, in the end, he'll lose his life for the loyalty not shown.
But, if he counts my cross worth more and loses life for me,
Then he'll receive, before my throne, a crown of victory.
My cross must be picked up each day and carried in one's heart
And used to counteract the sting of Satan's flaming dart.
The old self must be put away and never see the light
And this he can accomplish in my own great power and might.
Remember that I bore the cross and walked Golgotha's way;
I bore the crown of thorns as well and the deriding words they'd say.
My skin was torn and bleeding, and I was nailed upon that tree.
It is so little to compare when I say, "Follow me."
I do not promise life will be without its thorns and pain,
But if you yield up self to me, then on death, you'll live again.

THE ANGELS' SONGS

A chorus of angels witnessed creation's start
As God, to this earth, new life did impart.
They praised as the water divided the land
According to God's own magnificent plan.
Their eyes saw the dawn of the first sunrise bright.
They praised as the darkness discovered the light.
What anthems of praise for the great Sovereign God
Were offered to Him as the angels gave laud!

When the world's savior came down to earth.
The angelic choir sang of His earthly birth.
To the shepherds abiding in their fields at night,
They appeared in a glorious throng in the sky.
The news they proclaimed to the shepherds there
Was of a God-Man born in a stable so bare.
A babe that would save all of mankind from sin
If the lost would just open their hearts to Him.

They watched as the Savior hung on the cross,
As He bore willingly the sins of the lost.
No anthems were sung; their voices were stilled
When God turned away as Christ hung on that hill.
But when Christ rose in glory, the angels found voice
And at Christ's resurrection, they began to rejoice.
Their songs of rejoicing could only repeat
That death was defeated; it was Christ's victory.

When Christ comes to earth as a King, not a babe
The angels will sing of the price that was paid-
A King on a cross who had died and then rose,
A new life for those who Christ's narrow way chose.
They'll watch as all people, from all different worlds,
Will fall to their knees and proclaim Him as lord.
They'll sing loud hosannas to Jesus, their King.
What a great day to hear what the angels all sing!

THE DREAM

Today, all for Jesus, I tried sacrifice.
I put all the coins that would my coffee buy
In a box by my bedside. I had quite a pile!
I lay down my head with a satisfied smile.
I dreamed of a far land, cross oceans so wide,
I met missionaries, who knew some that had died
For daring to venture and spread God's own word.
It was hard to imagine. It seemed so absurd.
And yet as I listened, and heard each sad tale
I could not help but notice that each one, without fail,
Knew the risk they were taking and yet chose to go
Where they felt the Lord lead them, to fight the great foe.
Where their day-to-day living was entrusted to God
And each day could result in the shedding of blood.
But they knew that the Lord never left or forsaked,
To believe something else would not be their mistake.
And I watched as they shared God's great love with great joy
To each man, to each woman, to each girl and each boy.
And their love never wavered, never faltered or changed.
Those who do not know Christ would just say they're deranged.
But I heard as they prayed, with the tears flowing free
"Thank you, Jesus, my Lord, for your choosing of me
To help fight the fight that gives Satan no ease.
Help me, Lord, to stay true. Help me, Lord. Help me please."
When I woke and looked down at the coins near the bed,
I was shamed and embarrassed. The thought entered my head
That I'd thought I had made such a great sacrifice
When the others had been willing to give up their lives.
So, Dear Lord, help me daily to remember that dream
To give up what I ought to the missionary teams
'Til the whole human race has a chance to have heard
All the news of salvation that is found in your Word.

THE GARDENER AND THE VINE

I am the true vine and my Father is the gardener. He cuts off every branch in me that bears no fruit, while every branch that does bear fruit he prunes so that it will be even more fruitful...Remain in me, and I will remain in you. No branch can bear fruit by itself; it must remain in the vine. Neither can you bear fruit unless you remain in me.

John 15:1-2,4

You said, "My Father is the Gardener,
And I am the True Vine."
And when the branch does not bear fruit
God walks along the line
And cuts each branch, and cuts it clean.
'Twould seem a terrible thing to do.
But God knows best that after that
The branch would bear good fruit.

So, Lord, whene'er you watch my life
And find my purpose unfulfilled,
Then, Lord, cut deep and make the change
So I would do your will.
And let me take these awful cuts
That help to bear more fruit,
And help me to depend on you
'Til my growing time is through.

And as my life is daily spent
In the Vine I will remain
For the branch alone cannot bear fruit.
Your Word is clear and plain.
Apart from you, I'll surely die
And be cast into the fire.
But those that stay within the Vine
Will reach a goal much higher.

THE LIFE OF A SAVIOR

The day you came to earth, my Lord,
Was not proclaimed to all.
But to lowly shepherds, much afraid,
Who to their knees did fall.
When they had heard the angel's words
Of how you had been born
In the little town of Bethlehem
In a stable so forlorn,
They went to see the newborn king
That would die for fallen man.
They could not fully understand
God's rich redemption plan.
They ran and told all that they met
What the angel choir had said.
They could not help but tell good news
Of the King in manger bed.

You grew up in your Father's will,
And gave to all you met
The promise of a heavenly place
That they would not forget.
The blind could see, the lame could walk,
And the dead were raised to life.
By your word, you cast out demons
That were causing trial and strife.
Religious leaders of that time
All schemed throughout each day
To end your life and keep their power
That they saw ebbing away.
Then Judas came to them and told
That he'd identify:
"The man I kiss is Jesus Christ."
And they agreed that you must die.

They found you in the garden there,
Where you had prayed that night,
The soldiers in their armour
And the leaders in their delight.
Judas came and kissed your cheek,
And the soldiers took you away.
They led you to the courtyard where
You faced public disgrace.
"Are you the king of the Jews?" was asked.
"I am" was your reply.
"On a cloud from heaven, you will see
The Son of the God Most High."
They spat at you, and sneered your name.
They then blindfolded and beat you.
They jeered and yelled out "Prophesy".
They thought death was your due.

When Pilate asked the rowdy crowd,
"Which one will you see die?
Barrabas or this Jesus? Choose!"
"Give us Jesus! Crucify!"
They scourged and beat you then, my Lord,
'Til your blood ran in the street.
They crowned you with a thorny crown
That made their spectacle complete.
They nailed you to Golgotha's cross
And jeered your holy name.
They did not understand that you
Were the Son of God, as claimed.
You hung there, then you breathed your last.
"It is finished" you whispered low.
The soldier pierced your holy side
So the certainty of death they'd know.

They took you down and laid you in
The tomb, so dark and cold.
You lay there for three dark, dark days
As Scripture had foretold.

But then, you rose in majesty,
In divinity and power.
The rulers, who had caused your death,
Did not see your resurrection hour.
You rose and gained the victory
Over death and o'er the grave.
You had fulfilled your Father's plan
To have sin-filled, repentant hearts saved.
Because you came to earth, my Lord,
Because you died for me,
I will forever praise your name
Here on earth and for eternity.

THE SOLDIER AND THE SAVIOR

The soldier went about his task.
His goal was plain to see
He served his country how he could
To save democracy.
He never questioned why he chose
To do whatever he could;
He knew that Christ had told him to -
To augment others' good.
One day, when on a day patrol,
He saw the grenade land.
He knew he'd have to sacrifice
To save his comrade band.
He threw his body on the bomb
And willingly breathed his last
To save his mates from certain death.
His lot for Christ was cast.
And when I heard, I pondered
How the soldier mirrored Christ.
He too had surrendered his time on earth
And offered up his life.
The only difference I can see,
It's an important one I find
Is the soldier saved some kind of men
But Christ had saved mankind.
So, Friends, today on Remembrance Day,
I pray you'll realize
That to give one's life for others here
Will achieve a heavenly prize.
So thank a veteran here on earth
And pray for those who've past
Who gave so much so here this day
Our freedoms, forever, will last.

TRIUMPH AT THE TOMB

The world thought that it had won as Christ lay in the tomb.
And Satan wished to fill the world with doubt, despair and gloom.
He knew that, without any hope, the people would be lost.
He'd seen the world's champion nailed to the rugged cross.
He laughed and thought, "I have it all! I now hold all the power!"
He had not seen, and did not know, Christ's resurrection hour.
Christ lay within the tomb three days, then, as Scripture had foretold,
He rose in might and majesty, an awesome vision to behold!
And when Mary saw the gardener, she said, "Dear Sir, please say
Where they have put my Lord and King. Where does His body lay?"
She did not know the gardener was the one that she had sought,
The one who, by his own lifeblood, salvation thusly bought.
The gardener then said, "Mary", and Mary could then see
It was her Lord and Master, alive and whole and free.
Death had not won the victory; the grave's trophy had been lost,
For Christ's was resurrected after He paid Calvary's cost.
When her Savior stood before her, joy her sorrowing heart did fill
For she'd seen Him laying in the tomb, so lifeless and so still.
Like Mary, we can see now the power Christ displayed,
When He triumphed over death and won His victory o'er the grave.
That power is availed today when, with repentant heart,
A sinner gets a second birth and life with Jesus starts.
His victory over death ensures that we will win it too,
And we'll be blessed with love and peace, and with a life renewed.

WALKING IN THE WASTELAND

I'm walking in the desert, Lord.
I know you're by my side.
In day, I see a pillared cloud
And a pillared fire at night.
Your power is ever with me,
Availed for any trial.
My hand is in your hand, Lord,
As we walk each arid mile.
The jackals circle 'round me
And seek to do me harm.
I know you're right beside me
And I suffer no alarm.
I have your Living Water
In this dry and thirsty land
To cool me and sustain me
As I walk on sun-baked sand.
Your Word is my provision
For each day's trials and woes.
A feast of chapter, verse and line
That, to me, your love shows.
And I revel in communion
As we walk and as we speak
For I know the God of desert
Is the God of mountain's peak.
And I look, with expectation,
To the day when this will pass
And the dryness of the desert
Will transform to pasture's grass.
And I'll praise you for the moments
Spent in desert's searing heat
For I'll know that you provided
All this desert traveller's needs.

WHAT LOVE

What love was it that made you stay
Upon that Roman cross displayed?

What love was it that made you bear
The crown of thorns they made you wear?

What love said nothing when accused
So that salvation I'd not lose?

What love was it that made you leave
The heavenly realms? I can't conceive.

What love was it that bore the pain,
All suffered to remove sin's stain?

What love was it that knew the cost
And yet went forth to Calvary's cross?

What love was it that thought of me
While hanging on Golgotha's tree?

What love was buried for three days
Then rose in power to show the way?

What love was shown within that hour
Of resurrection, might and power?

And when I see Christ up above,
My only words: "What love! What love!"

WHEN I DREW NEAR TO CALVARY'S CROSS

When I drew near to Calvary's cross
My heart stained dark with sin,
You opened up your arms so wide
And welcomed me therein.

When I drew near to Calvary's cross
With trembling and with fear,
You held me in your open arms
And dried away each tear.

When I drew near to Calvary's cross
I sacrificed all my pride.
You opened up your loving arms
And took my gift inside.

When I drew near to Calvary's cross,
I brought no gift of worth.
You opened wide your arms of love
And gave abundant life on earth.

I know that when I walk your way
I will never suffer loss,
For you spread your arms out wide for me
When I drew near to Calvary's cross.

WHEN I NO LONGER WALK THIS EARTH

When I no longer walk this earth,
My soul will be set free.
I'll worship God and Christ, my King,
In glorious liberty.
My feet won't walk on concrete paths;
I'll walk on streets of gold.
I'll sing in praise to Christ, my Lord,
The glorious songs of old.
No pain will wrack this earthly shell;
A new body will be mine.
My mind won't dwell on scheduled lists
For heaven knows not time.
I will not miss loved ones gone on;
There'll be no broken hearts.
When I no longer walk this earth
And my heaven time will start.

When I no longer walk this earth,
I'll dwell in mansions grand,
Because I made a choice on earth
To follow God's own plan.
I'll never worry what to wear
For I'll wear Christ's righteousness,
With the victor's crown upon my head.
I could not hope for less.
No thirst or hunger will I know;
It's not in heaven's plan.
Instead I'll be an honoured guest
At the supper of the Lamb.
I'll drink the Living Water
And I'll eat the Bread of Life.
When I no longer walk this earth,
I'll escape life's toils and strife.

WHO ELSE?

No earthly king can chain your power,
Nor still your mighty hand.
No mortal knows the mind of God,
As you formulate your plans.

Who else can tell the ocean wide
How far to come to shore?
At your command, the wind does blow
And clouds their rain outpour.

Who else can know the thoughts of man,
Within their heart of hearts?
Who else created all the ways
That every life must start?

Each flower, bush and shady tree
Shows all your power and might,
As do the birds that fill the skies,
And the stars and moon at night.

Who else would love man in his sin,
And yield His life to show
That His great love would be the bridge
So, to heaven, we could go.

Who else is owed my love and praise?
Who else could own my heart?
None else, but God and Jesus Christ
Who, from me, will not depart.

I'll be availed of this great power
That man can't chain or still
As long as I abide in them,
And strive to do God's will.

WITH GOD ON THE HEIGHTS

"The Sovereign LORD is my strength; he makes my feet like the feet of a deer, he enables me to go on the heights."

Habakkuk 3:19 NIV

My strength lies in the Sovereign LORD.
I rest within His might.
He makes my feet the feet of deer;
With Him, I climb the heights.
No fear will enter in my soul;
My heart will know no dread.
For I know I don't climb alone;
By His hand, I am led.
My feet won't stumble; I can't fall;
My strength's in Him alone.
I'll jump from rock to craggy rock.
In me no fear'll be shown.
And what, from valley far below,
Looked impossible to climb
I now find unlike what I'd thought.
With ease, I pass the time.
God brought me to the mountaintop.
He knew my sure delight
In leaping from each rocky ledge,
Secure in His great might.
Secure that if I just retained
A sure grip on His hand,
My feet would never miss the mark
And safely I would land.
And in those days on valley floor,
I'll not forget the sights
That I could see from up on high
When with God, I climbed the heights.

WORDLESS WITNESS

He was a witness to many
Without speaking a word.
He just lived his life
And kept trusting the Lord.

His Bible, read daily,
Was more than enough
To continue the race
When the going got tough.

She spoke not a word
But she told of God's love
By her actions to others.
God's love she did prove.

She communioned with God
In His Word and in prayer.
No matter what happened,
She knew He'd be there.

Those around them all noticed
That they weren't the same –
They never quarreled or angered
Never profaned the Lord's Name.

Their lives were their witness,
And though it may seem absurd,
They both witnessed to many
Without speaking a word.

YOU ARE WITH ME

When all my world is crumbling down,
And I'm about to fall,
I know that I will rest secure
If on your name I call.

No power upon this earth can win
Whenever you are near.
I know within my heart of hearts
Your love for me is clear.

I know your grace will be poured out
No matter circumstance.
I know that you will hold my hand
Each step of my life's dance.

So, Lord, I pray each morning new
That I'll look and I'll see
You standing right there by my side.
My praise will rise to Thee.

I'll sing a song of faithfulness
That you have shown each day.
I'll praise you for your mercy, Lord,
As I walk your narrow way.

And in those times when words won't come
Then, Lord, look in my heart
And know I know your love for me
Is true and won't depart.

So thank you, Lord, for all your love
Your grace and mercy, too.
The greatest choice I ever made
Was to yield my life to you.